My New Friend

By Jillian Powell

Photography by Chris Fairclough

WAYLAND

First published in 2011 by Wayland

Wayland
338 Euston Road
London NW1 3BH

Wayland Australia
Level 17/207 Kent Street
Sydney, NSW 2000

Editor, Wayland: Julia Adams
Produced for Wayland by Discovery Books Ltd
Managing editor: Rachel Tisdale
Project editor: Colleen Ruck
Designer: Ian Winton
Photography: Chris Fairclough
Consultant: Helen Beale (Teacher and Library Coordinator,
Robert Le Kyng Primary School, Swindon)

The author and photographer would like to acknowledge the
following for their help in preparing this book: Clementine, Adelina,
Haniya Lampkin-Berry, Mr and Mrs Lampkin-Berry; Emily, Megan,
Mr and Mrs Robinson; Headteacher Jane Johnson, staff and pupils
at Norton Primary School.

British Library Cataloguing in Publication Data
Powell, Jillian.
  My new friend.
  1. Friendship--Pictorial works--Juvenile literature.
  I. Title
  302.3'4-dc22

ISBN: 978 0 7502 6286 6

Printed in China

Wayland is a division of Hachette Children's Books, an Hachette UK company.
www.hachette.co.uk

Contents

My home

My name is Clementine. I live with my mum and dad and my two little sisters, Adelina and Haniya.

I share a bedroom with my little sister Adelina. We like to play together in our bedroom.

Neighbours

Emily and her family have just moved into a house down the road. I met Emily when we were both out on our bikes. She is my new **friend**.

I am **excited** because Emily is going to the same school as me. It is the first day back after the holidays.

Our mums walk to school with us.

Classmates

Emily is in the same class as me. Our class teacher, Miss Cundick, says we can sit next to each other. We write about what we did in the holidays.

After school, Mum comes to pick me up. She has been chatting to Emily's mum while she waited for me.

Visiting Emily

Emily has asked me to play at her house after school. Mum takes me there.

Emily says we can play in the garden.

Emily shows me her dog, Poppy. Poppy's fur feels very soft. She is really cute.

Playing together

Today Emily comes back to my house for tea. We have pizza with my sister Adelina.

After tea we play one of my **favourite** games.

Emily has not played it before, but she really enjoys it. We both want to win!

Not friends?

In the playground at school today, Emily plays a clapping game with Sophie.

I want to join in, but Emily says I don't know the game.

When it is time for our PE lesson, Emily picks Sophie as her **partner**.

I feel sad because I don't think Emily wants to be my friend any more.

Together again

After school, Emily comes round to say she is sorry if she upset me. She still wants to be my friend.

It's nice to be friends again. Mum says it is okay to have lots of other friends, too.

Emily teaches me how to play the clapping game. It doesn't take me long to learn it!

Emily's birthday

It is Emily's birthday next week. I make a **friendship bracelet** for her.

I pick all her favourite colours.

I make a birthday card for
Emily, too. I draw flowers
on it because I know
she likes them.

The party

Today is Emily's birthday and she is having a party. We all sit down for some party food.

Then I give Emily her friendship bracelet. She loves it. Emily says I am her best friend. She is my best friend, too!

Glossary

excited feeling happy and looking forward to something.

favourite something you like best of all.

friend someone you like to spend time with.

friendship bracelet a bracelet that you give to someone as a sign of friendship.

partner someone you pair up with.

Further information

Books

Thoughts and Feelings: Making Friends by Sarah Levete (Franklin Watts, 2007)

Healthy and Happy: Family and Friends by Louise Spilsbury (Wayland, 2009)

A First Look At: Respect For Others – Everybody Matters by Pat Thomas (Wayland, 2010)

Websites

www.bbc.co.uk/cbbc/bugbears
An interactive website that provides advice about friends and friendships.

www.cyh.com
The Kids' Health section of this website includes helpful facts and information about topics such as making friends and friendships.

www.kidshealth.org/kid/feeling
This website includes practical information about dealing with thoughts and feelings such as feeling shy.

Things to do

Literacy/Speaking and Listening
Write down two single words that best describe your new friend. You can discuss your choices with your friend and the rest of your class.

Art
Make a collage of pictures of your friend's favourite things. Cut out lots of different pictures from newspapers and magazines and stick them onto coloured card. Your friend will love it!

Index

My New

Contents of titles in series:

Childminder
978 0 7502 6288 0

My family
My new childminder
After school
At the park
Playing indoors
Arts and crafts
Dinner time
Having fun
Home with Mum

Friend
978 0 7502 6286 6

My home
Neighbours
Classmates
Visiting Emily
Playing together
Not friends?
Together again
Emily's birthday
The party

Sister
978 0 7502 6285 9

My family
Shopping for baby
Getting ready
Mum goes to hospital
My sister Holly
Helping out
At home with my sister
Playtime
Bath and bedtime

Dad
978 0 7502 6287 3

My family
Moving in
Changes
Helping us
Kevin's son
Weekends
Family arguments
Having fun
My step-family

School
978 0 7502 6284 2

My first day at school
My class
Assembly
Paint and play
Snack time
Reading and writing
Lunch
Circle time
Going home

WAYLAND

I Know Someone with Diabetes

Vic Parker

www.raintreepublishers.co.uk
Visit our website to find out
more information about
Raintree books.

To order:
☎ Phone 0845 6044371
🖨 Fax +44 (0) 1865 312263
💻 Email myorders@raintreepublishers.co.uk

Customers from outside the UK please telephone +44 1865 312262

Raintree is an imprint of Capstone Global Library
Limited, a company incorporated in England and
Wales having its registered office at 7 Pilgrim Street,
London, EC4V 6LB – Registered company number:
6695582

Text © Capstone Global Library Limited 2011
First published in hardback in 2011
The moral rights of the proprietor have been asserted.

Edited by Rebecca Rissman, Daniel Nunn
  and Siân Smith
Designed by Joanna Hinton Malivoire
Picture research by Mica Brancic
Originated by Capstone Global Library
Printed and bound in China by Leo Paper Products Ltd

ISBN 978 1 406 22076 6
15 14 13 12 11
10 9 8 7 6 5 4 3 2 1

British Library Cataloguing in Publication Data
Parker, Victoria.
I know someone with diabetes. – (Understanding
health issues)
  1. Diabetes–Juvenile literature.
  I. Title II. Series
  616.4'62-dc22

Acknowledgements
We would like to thank the following for permission to
reproduce photographs: Alamy pp. 15 (© ACE Stock
Limited), 16 (© Anne-Marie Palmer), 17 (© Martin
Shields); Getty Images pp. 18 (PhotoAlto Agency RF
Collections/Odilon Dimier), 27 (AFP Photo/Thomas
Coex); Getty Images Entertainment p. 26 (Jemal
Countess); iStockphoto pp. 6 (© Steve Debenport),
13 (© Aldo Murillo), 20 (© Cristian Lazzari), 21 (©
Christopher Futcher), 23 (© Radu Razvan); Photolibrary
pp. 4 (Radius Images), 5 (Uppercut Images RF/
Jay Reilly), 7 (Photoalto/Laurence Mouton), 8 (age
fotostock/Javier Larrea), 9 (imagebroker.net/Martin
Moxter), 10 (OJO Images/Sam Edwards), 11 (Banana
Stock), 14 (BSIP Medical/May May), 19 (Index Stock
Imagery/Robert Ginn), 22 (BSIP Medical/Jose Oto), 25
(Image Source); Shutterstock p. 12 (© Maga).

Cover photograph of a couple and their daughter
cooking reproduced with permission of Getty Images
(Photodisc/Jack Hollingsworth).

We would like to thank Matthew Siegel and Ashley
Wolinski for their invaluable help in the preparation of
this book.

Every effort has been made to contact copyright
holders of any material reproduced in this book. Any
omissions will be rectified in subsequent printings if
notice is given to the publisher.

Contents

Some words are printed in bold, **like this**. You can
find out what they mean in the glossary.

Do you know someone with diabetes?

You might have a friend with diabetes mellitus, often just called 'diabetes'. Diabetes is a **medical condition**. This means that the doctor has given your friend things to do to stay healthy.

You cannot catch diabetes.

4

Someone with diabetes can wear a bracelet or necklace to let others know.

You cannot tell that someone has diabetes just by looking at them. There is nothing to see. This is because diabetes happens on the inside of someone's body, not the outside.

What is Type 1 diabetes?

When we eat, our bodies make something inside us called **insulin**. Insulin helps turn the sugar we get from certain foods into **energy**, so we can run and jump and play.

Sugar comes from foods such as bread, bananas, sweets, and pasta.

Too much sugar in your blood can make you feel very tired, thirsty, and unwell.

When a young person gets Type 1 diabetes, their body stops making insulin. This means their body cannot turn sugar from their food into energy. Instead, the sugar builds up in their blood and makes them unwell.

How do you get Type 1 diabetes?

No one is sure why young people get Type 1 diabetes. Some children who develop it have an older relative with Type 1 diabetes too. Others suddenly get it after a nasty illness.

Many scientists are working to discover what causes Type 1 diabetes.

Young people with diabetes can join groups or go on breaks where they can have fun and meet other people with diabetes.

Most young people who get Type 1 diabetes are between the ages of 10 and 14. However, some are even younger. Once you get Type 1 diabetes, you have it for the rest of your life.

A different type of diabetes

Many more adults than young people get diabetes. Adults usually develop a different type of the **medical condition**. This is called Type 2 diabetes.

Many people have grandparents with Type 2 diabetes.

A person with Type 2 diabetes still makes **insulin** in their body. However, this insulin either does not work as well as it should, or there is not enough of it.

Sugar can build up in the blood of someone with Type 2 diabetes, just as it can for someone with Type 1 diabetes.

The causes of Type 2 diabetes

Exercising and eating healthily can help everyone to stay well.

Adults can get Type 2 diabetes if they are overweight. This is often because they have made unhealthy food choices and have not taken regular exercise.

Adults are more likely to get Type 2 diabetes if other people in their family have it too. People from certain **ethnic** backgrounds, such as Afro-Caribbean, South-Asian, or Hispanic, are also more likely to develop Type 2 diabetes.

You might be surprised by how many grown-ups you know who have Type 2 diabetes.

Living with Type 1 diabetes

Someone with Type 1 diabetes needs to take **insulin** as medicine. Then their body can turn the sugar from food into **energy** and they feel well. They have up to five **injections** of insulin every day.

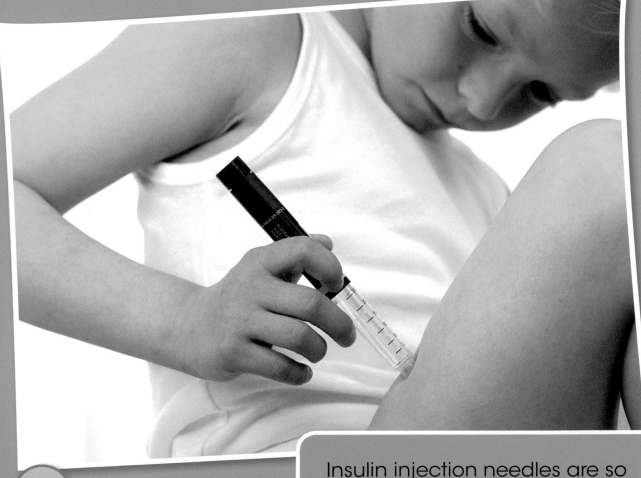

Insulin injection needles are so small you can hardly feel them.

Wearing an insulin pump will not hurt the person wearing it.

Other people with Type 1 diabetes use an insulin pump. This clips onto their clothes while a tiny needle stays in their skin. You can sleep, shower, and even swim wearing an insulin pump.

Living with Type 2 diabetes

Many people with Type 2 diabetes can take tablets as treatment. These tablets either get the body to make enough **insulin**, or help the body's insulin to work better.

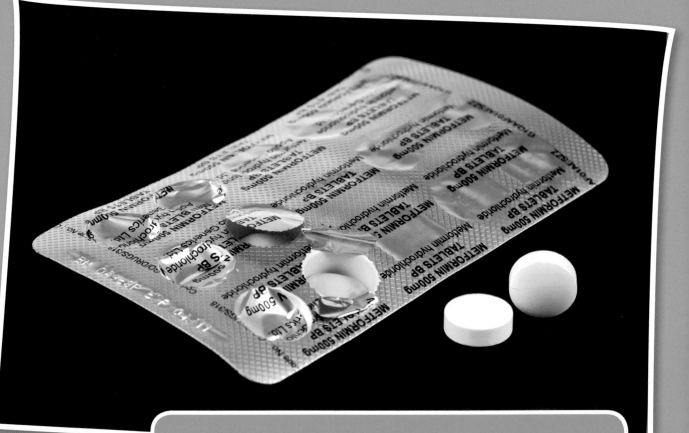

You can help a friend with Type 2 diabetes by reminding them to take their tablets.

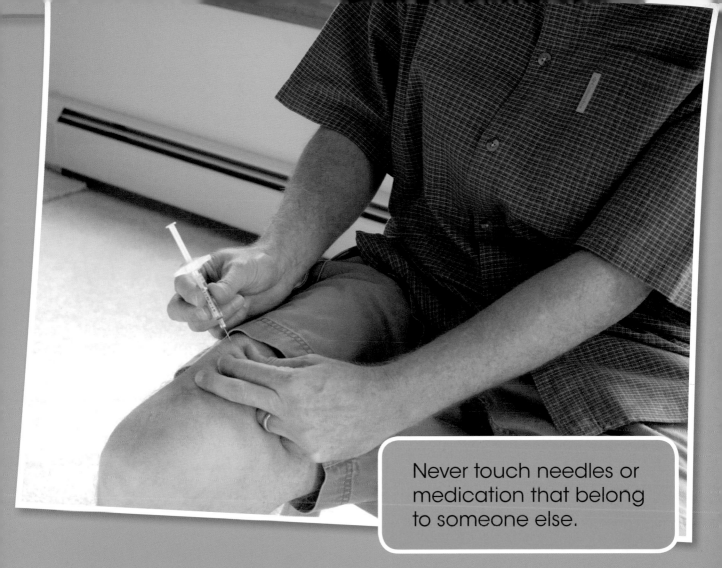

Never touch needles or medication that belong to someone else.

Some people with Type 2 diabetes have **injections**. These may be of a medicine that works the same way that tablets do. Or they may be injections of insulin.

What is a hypo?

Sometimes, someone with diabetes may turn pale, shaky, confused, and grumpy. This is because all the sugar from their food has been turned into **energy** and used up. It is called having a **hypo**.

You may realize that a friend with diabetes is having a hypo before they do.

Someone having a hypo needs a sugary drink or some sugary sweets straight away. They should soon feel better. If they do not, you can help by calling an ambulance urgently.

If someone having a hypo does not have sugar quickly enough, they may pass out and have a **seizure**.

Food choices

To stay well, people with diabetes should eat regular, small amounts of starchy food at meal and snack times. Starchy foods include potatoes, rice, pasta, and bread.

Bananas are a tasty starchy food.

We should all make healthy food choices to stay well.

People with diabetes should usually avoid sugary foods, but eat lots of vegetables and **wholefoods**. They should not skip meals or their healthy snacks. People without diabetes should also do these things to eat healthily.

21

About blood testing

If someone with diabetes does not follow their doctor's instructions, the amount of sugar in their blood may rise too high. This can harm different body parts, such as their eyes and **nerves**.

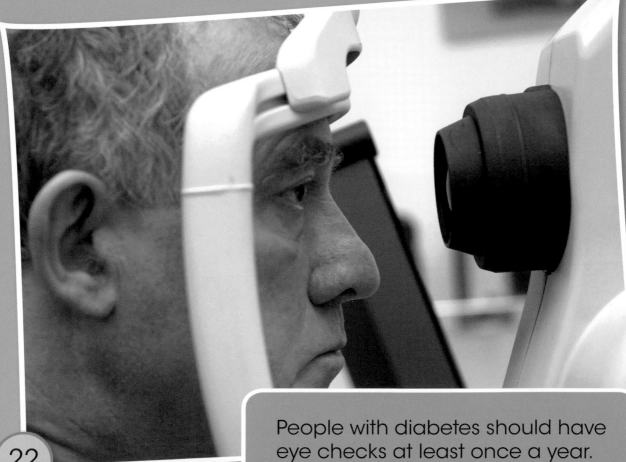

People with diabetes should have eye checks at least once a year.

You can help a friend with diabetes write down their test results to show their doctor.

A person with diabetes can check how much sugar is in their blood by using a special machine. This can help them to keep their blood sugar level just right, so they stay healthy.

Being a good friend

There are many ways you can be a good friend to someone with diabetes. You can:

- try not to think of your friend as 'ill'

- help each other to exercise

- carry a sugary drink in case your friend has a **hypo**

- make healthy food choices with your friend.

We all have different bodies and different personalities.

Living with diabetes can be difficult at times. We are all different in many ways. A good friend likes us and values us for who we are.

Famous people with diabetes

Nick Jonas wears an **insulin** pump to manage his diabetes.

Nick Jonas got Type 1 diabetes at the age of 13. It hasn't stopped him becoming a popular singer and actor with his own TV show.

Many people say that Steve Redgrave is the greatest ever Olympic athlete.

Steve Redgrave was already a champion rower when he developed Type 1 diabetes. He worked hard to manage the **medical condition** and won gold medals at five Olympic Games!

Diabetes – facts and fiction

Facts

- At least 171 million people in the world have diabetes.

- Experts guess that half a million people have Type 2 diabetes without knowing it yet.

Fiction

(?) Eating lots of diabetic sweets and chocolate is a good idea.

WRONG! 'Diabetic' foods can still raise blood sugar and can give you tummy-ache and diarrhoea.

(?) People with diabetes should never eat sugary foods and drinks.

WRONG! People with diabetes may need to eat some sugary stuff at certain times, such as if they exercise, or if they are having a **hypo**.

Glossary

energy power to do something. We use energy when we run, jump, and play.

ethnic belonging to a certain race of people

hypo short for 'hypoglycaemia', which means 'low blood sugar' (not enough sugar in someone's blood)

injection people use an injection to take medicine into their bodies through a needle

insulin liquid made in our bodies which controls the amount of sugar in our blood

medical condition health problem that a person has for a long time or for life

nerves long, fine threads that carry information between body parts and the brain

seizure disturbance in someone's brain, which can affect their senses, behaviour, feelings, or thoughts for a while

wholefood food that is kept as natural as possible, without having things added or taken away from it

Find out more

Books to read

Diabetes (Feeling Ill?), Jillian Powell (Evans Brothers, 2007)

Juvenile Diabetes (First Facts), Jason Glaser (First Facts Books, 2006)

What Does it Mean to Have Diabetes?, Louise Spilsbury (Heinemann Library, 2003)

Websites

kidshealth.org/kid/centers/diabetes_center.html

Watch an animation that helps you learn about Type 1 and Type 2 diabetes on this website.

www.diabetes.org.uk/Guide-to-diabetes/Food_and_recipes

This part of the Diabetes UK's website has recipes and information on healthy eating for people who have diabetes.

Index